The Book of Revelation

STUDY GUIDE

Jerome Kodell, O.S.B.

Little Rock
Scripture Study Program

THE LITURGICAL PRESS
St. John's Abbey
Collegeville, Minnesota 56321

DIOCESE OF LITTLE ROCK
2415 North Tyler Street
P.O. Box 7239, Forest Park Station
LITTLE ROCK, ARKANSAS 72217

Telephone
Area Code 501
664-0340

Office of the Bishop

Dear Friend,

We Catholics have always believed that the Lord is present in his Word, in his sacrament, and through baptism and confirmation in each one of us. In post-Vatican II times, the emphasis upon Jesus in his Word among us has grown and deepened. In many parts of our country, Scripture study programs have become effective instruments for the deepening of our spiritual life.

Some years ago I encouraged our people to embrace God's holy Word. I used the words of Our Lord to St. Augustine, "Take and read." I asked that the Scriptures be prayerfully read. The Little Rock Scripture Study Program provided the way. Out of this program has come an enrichment of our spiritual life and a deeper and closer relationship to the Lord.

The pages of this study guide lay down the challenge to you, the reader. The Word of God can take root in your soul; the Word of God can change your life. The Word of God can make you a saint.

Your friend,

✝ Andrew J. McDonald

✝Andrew J. McDonald
Bishop of Little Rock

Sacred Scripture

"The Church has always venerated the divine Scriptures just as she venerates the body of the Lord, since from the table of both the word of God and of the body of Christ she unceasingly receives and offers to the faithful the bread of life, especially in the sacred liturgy. She has always regarded the Scriptures together with sacred tradition as the supreme rule of faith, and will ever do so. For, inspired by God and committed once and for all to writing, they impart the word of God Himself without change, and make the voice of the Holy Spirit resound in the words of the prophets and apostles. Therefore, like the Christian religion itself, all the preaching of the Church must be nourished and ruled by sacred Scripture. For in the sacred books, the Father who is in heaven meets His children with great love and speaks with them; and the force and power in the word of God is so great that it remains the support and energy of the Church, the strength of faith for her sons, the food of the soul, the pure and perennial source of spiritual life."

Vatican II, Dogmatic Constitution on Divine Revelation, no. 21.

INTERPRETATION OF SACRED SCRIPTURE

"Since God speaks in sacred Scripture through men in human fashion, the interpreter of sacred Scripture, in order to see clearly what God wanted to communicate to us, should carefully investigate what meaning the sacred writers really intended, and what God wanted to manifest by means of their words.

"Those who search out the intention of the sacred writers must, among other things, have regard for 'literary forms.' For truth is proposed and expressed in a variety of ways, depending on whether a text is history of one kind or another, or whether its form is that of prophecy, poetry, or some other type of speech. The interpreter must investigate what meaning the sacred writer intended to express and actually expressed in particular circumstances as he used contemporary literary forms in accordance with the situation of his own time and culture. For the correct understanding of what the sacred author wanted to assert, due attention must be paid to the customary and characteristic styles of perceiving, speaking, and narrating which prevailed at the

time of the sacred writer, and to the customs men normally followed at that period in their everyday dealings with one another."
Vatican II, Dogmatic Constitution on Divine Revelation, no. 12.

Instructions

MATERIALS FOR THE STUDY

This Study Guide: The Book of Revelation

Bible: The New American Bible with Revised New Testament or The New Jerusalem Bible is recommended. Paraphrased editions are discouraged as they offer little if any help when facing difficult textual questions. Choose a Bible you feel free to write in or underline.

Commentary: The Collegeville Bible Commentary: New Testament Series, volume 11, *The Book of Revelation* by Pheme Perkins (The Liturgical Press), is used with this study. The abbreviation for this commentary, CBC-NT volume 11, and the assigned pages are found at the beginning of each lesson.

ADDITIONAL MATERIALS

Bible Dictionary: *The Dictionary of the Bible* by John L. McKenzie, (Macmillan) is highly recommended as an additional reference.

Notebook: A notebook may be useful for lecture notes and your personal reflections.

WEEKLY LESSONS

Lesson 1—Rev 1
Lesson 2—Rev 2–3
Lesson 3—Rev 4–6
Lesson 4—Rev 7–9
Lesson 5—Rev 10–11

Lesson 6—Rev 12–14
Lesson 7—Rev 15–17
Lesson 8—Rev 18–20
Lesson 9—Rev 21–22

YOUR DAILY PERSONAL STUDY

The first step is prayer. Open your heart and mind to God. Reading Scripture is an opportunity to listen to God who loves you. Pray that the same Holy Spirit who guided the formation of Scripture will inspire you to correctly understand what you read and empower you to make what you read a part of your life.

The next step is commitment. Daily spiritual food is as necessary as food for the body. This study is divided into daily units. Schedule a regular time and place for your study, as free from distractions as possible. Allow about twenty minutes a day. Make it a daily appointment with God.

As you begin each lesson read the assigned chapters of Scripture found at the beginning of each lesson, the footnotes in your Bible, and then the indicated pages of the commentary. This preparation will give you an overview of the entire lesson and help you to appreciate the context of individual passages.

As you reflect on Scripture, ask yourself these four questions:

1. *What does the Scripture passage say?*
   Read the passage slowly and reflectively. Use your imagination to picture the scene or enter into it.

2. *What does the Scripture passage mean?*
   Read the footnotes and the commentary to help you understand what the sacred writers intended and what God wanted to communicate by means of their words.

3. *What does the Scripture passage mean to me?*
   Meditate on the passage. God's Word is living and powerful. What is God saying to you today? How does the Scripture passage apply to your life today?

4. *What am I going to do about it?*
   Try to discover how God may be challenging you in this passage. An encounter with God contains a challenge to know God's will and follow it more closely in daily life.

THE QUESTIONS ASSIGNED FOR EACH DAY

Read the questions and references for each day. The questions are designed to help you listen to God's Word and to prepare you for the weekly small-group discussion.

Some of the questions can be answered briefly and objectively by referring to the Bible references and the commentary *(What does the passage say?)*. Some will lead you to a better understanding of how the Scriptures apply to the Church, sacraments, and society *(What does the passage mean?)*. Some questions will invite you to consider how God's Word challenges or supports you in your relationships with God and others *(What does the passage mean to me?)*. Finally, the questions will lead you to examine your actions in light of Scripture *(What am I going to do about it?)*.

Write your responses in this study guide or in a notebook to help you clarify and organize your thoughts and feelings.

THE WEEKLY SMALL-GROUP MEETING

The weekly small-group sharing is the heart of the Little Rock Scripture Study Program. Participants gather in small groups to share the results of praying, reading and reflecting on Scripture and on the assigned questions. The goal of the discussion is for group members to be strengthened and nourished individually and as a community through sharing how God's Word speaks to them and affects their daily lives. The daily study questions will guide the discussion; it is not necessary to discuss all the questions.

All members share the responsibility of creating an atmosphere of loving support and trust in the group by respecting the opinions and experiences of others, and by affirming and encouraging one another. The simple shared prayer which begins and ends each small group meeting also helps create the open and trusting environment in which group members can share their faith deeply and grow in the study of God's Word.

A distinctive feature of this program is its emphasis on and trust in God's presence working in and through each member. Sharing responses to God's presence in the Word and in others can bring about remarkable growth and transformation.

THE WRAP-UP LECTURE

The lecture is designed to develop and clarify the themes of the lesson. It is not intended to form the basis for the group discussion. For this reason the lecture is always held at the end of the meeting. If several small groups meet at one time, the large group will gather together in a central location to listen to the lecture.

Lectures may be given by a local speaker. They are also available on audio- or video-cassette.

LESSON 1   Rev 1
CBC-NT volume 11, pages 5–19

Day 1

1. a) What do you expect to find in the Book of Revelation?
   b) What apprehensions do you have about studying this book?

2. What was the occasion of the composition of the Book of Revelation?

3. Who is the author and where is he at the time of writing (1:1, 9)?

Day 2

4. How is the term "revelation" used in 1:1?

5. What is the overall tone of the seven "beatitudes" found throughout the Book of Revelation: 1:3; 14:3; 16:15; 19:9; 20:6; 22:7, 14?

6. In what ways are you called to be a "faithful witness" (1:5). (See 2:13; Acts 1:8; 1 Pet 2:11-12; 3:15-17.)

Day 3

7. What does it mean that we are a kingdom of priests (1:6)? (See Exod 19:6; Rom 12:1; 1 Pet 2:9.)

8. How is the oracle in 1:7 both good and bad news?

9. Why are these seven Churches and no others addressed (1:11)?

Day 4

10. Read Dan 7:13-14 and show how it can be applied to Jesus.

11. What is indicated by the robe and golden sash (1:13)? (See Exod 28:6-8; Lev 16:32.)

12. What is the significance of Jesus holding seven stars (1:16, 20)?

Day 5

13. The image of Jesus in 1:13-16 appeals to the senses and to the imagination. What visual images of Jesus appeal to you?

14. a) What is the sharp, two-edged sword (1:16)? (See Eph 6:17; Heb 4:12.)
    b) How have you felt this sword in your life?

15. a) How do Jesus' words give hope to the persecuted Christian (1:17-18)? (See John 5:21.)
    b) When have you felt most persecuted or fearful? (See Pss 3; 17:6-12.)

Day 6

16. How does John's vision (1:12-16) give evidence of Jesus' presence in the Church (1:20)? (See Acts 9:5; 1 Cor 12:7.)

17. Where in the Church today is the message of reassurance most needed?

LESSON 2   Rev 2–3
CBC-NT volume 11, pages 19–26

Day 1

1. Based on the discussion or lecture from the first lesson, what insight will help you in your study of Revelation?

2. a) Name a strong point and a weak point of the Ephesian community (2:1-7).
   b) Have you ever experienced the same weakness? How did you recover in this area?

3. a) What was the teaching of the Nicolaitans (2:6, 15)?
   b) What would be a Nicolaitan attitude today?

Day 2

4. a) What is meant by saying to the Church of Smyrna "you are rich" (2:9)?
   b) In what ways do you share in this richness?

5. a) What is the "second death" (2:11)? (See 20:6, 14; 21:8.)
   b) Who is the "victor" (2:11)? (See 2:7, 17, 26; 3:5, 12, 21.)

6. What is meant by "Satan's throne" at Pergamum (2:13)?

Day 3

7. Describe a contemporary "faithful witness" for Christ (2:13). (See Heb 12:1.)

8. How are the hidden manna and the new name expressions of Jesus' special relationship to each Christian (2:17)? (See 3:12; Isa 62:2.)

9. Could your parish community be identified by the attributes listed in 2:19? Give examples.

Day 4

10. What is significant about the victor receiving "the morning star" (2:28)?

11. How can one appear to be alive but instead be dead (1:1)? Give examples.

12. How has Sardis failed to stay on guard (3:2-3)?

Day 5

13. The people of Sardis are admonished to be watchful (3:2-3). What are common signs of drifting and drowsiness among Christians? (See 2 Pet 2:20-22.)

14. Why is the color white often used in the Book of Revelation (3:4-5)? (See 2:17; 3:18; 6:9-11; 7:13-14; 19:11-14.)

15. How is the "open door" promise a source of hope (3:8)? (See Isa 22:22; Acts 14:27.)

Day 6

16. How does the idea of Jesus' coming affect your life (3:11)?

17. a) How does Laodicea's geographical situation affect the message about lukewarmness (3:15-16)?
    b) What would be an example of "lukewarmness" in the faith (3:16)?

18. What does 3:20 mean for your spiritual life?

LESSON 3 Rev 4–6
CBC-NT volume 11, pages 26–38

Day 1

1. In last week's lesson, the vision addressed to which city most impressed you? Why?

2. a) Why does the vision begin with a description of the divine throne or court (4:1-8)?
   b) After reading both the Scripture text and the commentary, what part of the description best demonstrates to you the image of God prevalent at the time?

3. Who do the twenty-four elders represent (4:4)? (See Gen 49; Luke 6:12-16; 22:28-30.)

Day 2

4. Trace the biblical background of the "sea of glass" (4:6). (See Exod 24:10; 1 Kgs 7:23-26; Ps 104:3; Ezek 1:22-26.)

5. What do the four living creatures manifest about God's rule (4:6-8)? (See Ezek 1:5-21.)

6. What are some of the liturgical elements in 4:8-11?

Day 3

7. Why is the scroll sealed (5:1)? (See Isa 29:11; Ezek 2:10; Dan 12:4.)

8. How had the Lamb won the right to open the scroll with the seven seals (5:5-10)? (See 1 Pet 1:18-19.)

9. What is symbolized by the Lamb standing though slain (5:6)? (See John 1:29.)

Day 4

10. Why do you suppose that the title "Lamb" is the one most frequently used in Revelation to speak of Christ (5:6)? (See 7:9; 14:1, 4; 21:9; 22:1-3.)

11. What is the significance of God creating a kingdom out of "every tribe and tongue, people and nation" (5:9-10)? (See Mark 16:15.)

12. The "prayers of the holy ones" were offered to the Lamb with incense (5:8). (See 8:4.) When are you reminded that the saints intercede on your behalf?

Day 5

13. What is the major difference between the four horsemen of Zechariah (1:8-11; 6:1-6) and those of Revelation (6:1-9)?

14. Which enemy of the Romans is symbolized by the rider on the white horse (6:2)? (See 9:14-19.)

15. Why does the rider of the black horse hold a pair of scales (6:5)? (See Lev 26:26.)

Day 6

16. How would you describe the mood or tone of the martyrs in heaven (6:9-11)? (See Job 16:18.)

17. Can you think of any event that might be described as graphically as the earthquake in 6:12-17?

18. a) Which image in chapter 6 might have been most threatening to the people at the time?
    b) What are the images of judgment that come to your mind? Are these hopeful or despairing?

LESSON 4   Rev 7–9
CBC-NT volume 11, pages 38–44

Day 1

1. What lesson from last week's lecture has remained with you?

2. a) How is the imagery of sealing used in the Old Testament (7:2)? (See Gen 4:15; Exod 28:11; Isa 44:5; Ezek 9:4.)
   b) How are Christians sealed sacramentally?

3. What is symbolized by the 144,000 "marked with the seal" (7:3-4)? (See 14:1-5.)

Day 2

4. How are the palms in 7:9 like those mentioned in John 12:12-13?

5. a) What is meant by surviving the "time of great distress" (7:14)?
   b) In what ways can our time be described as a time of distress?

6. What is "life-giving water" (7:17)? (See 21:6; Isa 49:10; 55:1; Ezek 47:1-12; John 4:10-14.)

Day 3

7. Revelation includes several descriptions of salvation (7:15-17; 21:9-27). Write your own description to share with the group.

8. a) What is the meaning of incense (8:3)? (See 5:8; Exod 30:1.)
   b) How is it used today in the Church?

9. Which plagues of Egypt are alluded to in trumpets 1 and 4 (8:7, 12)? (See Exod 9:23-26; 10:21-23.)

Day 4

10. What event of the time might be alluded to in the image of the mountain being cast into the sea (8:8)? (See Jer 51:25.)

11. What is meant by "wormwood" (8:11)? (See Jer 9:14; 23:15.)

12. Do the first four trumpets announce the final destruction (8:7-13)?

Day 5

13. Read the description of the locust plague in Joel 1–2. What similarities and differences are there with this present description (9:3-11)?

14. How can the description of the locusts (9:3-11) serve to prevent only literal interpretations of Revelation?

15. a) How does one receive the seal of God (9:4)?
    b) Are the effects of being sealed always present in a Christian?

Day 6

16. What is the English equivalent of the names of the angel of the abyss (9:11)?

17. How is the response of the people in 9:20-21 like that of Pharaoh in Exod 9:12, 34?

18. What are the indications of conversion in the people of the world today?

LESSON 5   Rev 10–11
CBC-NT volume 11, pages 44–50

Day 1

1. In the study so far, what has most impressed you about the Book of Revelation?

2. How does the mighty angel of 10:1 resemble the One who sent him? (See 4:2-3.)

3. What is the significance of the thunder and the lion's roar (10:3)? (See Joel 4:16; Amos 1:2; 3:8.)

Day 2

4. Why is the message of the seven thunders sealed up (10:4)?

5. a) What is meant by saying the scroll will be sweet in the mouth but sour in the stomach (10:8-10)?
   b) Read Ezek 3:1-4. In what ways have you seen God's message "consumed" in your own day?
   c) Give examples of how the Word of God serves both to chastise and to enliven.

6. What is meant for Christians by God's temple and altar (11:1)? (See 21:2-3; Ezek 40:1-5; Zech 2:5-9.)

Day 3

7. Why are the temple and altar measured (11:1)? (See Ezek 40:1-5.)

8. Review the following texts as background for 11:2-3: 1 Kgs 17:1; Dan 7:25; 12:7; 1 Macc 1:20-24; Luke 4:25. What meanings do you find for 3½ years, 42 months, or 1,260 days?

9. a) Why are the two witnesses wearing sackcloth (11:3)? (See 1 Chr 21:16-17; Isa 15:3; Matt 11:21.)
   b) How do we demonstrate the same attitude today?

Day 4

10. Which Old Testament figures are glimpsed in the two witnesses (11:4-6)? (See 1 Kgs 17:1; Zech 4:3-14.)

11. What is meant by the beast from the abyss (11:7)? (See 13:1; 17:8; Dan 7:3.)

12. a) What do Sodom and Egypt stand for in biblical history (11:8)? (See Gen 13:13; Exod 3:7; Isa 3:9.)
    b) Where are there Sodoms and Egypts today?

Day 5

13. a) Why are the corpses of the two wtinesses not allowed to be buried (11:9)? (See Deut 28:26; Isa 66:24; Jer 14:16.)
    b) What broad similarities can you find between the ministry of the two witnesses and the ministry of Jesus (11:3-12)? (See Luke 24:50-53; Acts 10:38-43.)

14. What causes you to respect some witnesses as prophets and not others? (See Deut 13:2-5.)

15. a) What is the motivation for worship in 11:13?
    b) What other motivations have you observed?

Day 6

16. Does the hymn in 11:17-18 refer to time within the world's history or to the time after judgment?

17. What is the significance of the violent signs of nature surrounding the ark of the covenant (11:19)?

LESSON 6   Rev 12–14
CBC-NT volume 11, pages 50–62

Day 1

1. What insight did you gain from last week's discussion or lecture?

2. Who are represented by the mother and child (12:1-6)? (See Gen 3:15; Song 6:10; Isa 66:7-13.)

3. What is the significance of the woman wearing a "crown of twelve stars" (12:1)? (See Sir 44:23.)

Day 2

4. How could 12:6 be a source of comfort to the persecuted Christians? (See Exod 16:32; 35-36; Amos 2:10.)

5. a) What is symbolized by the war between Michael and the dragon (12:7-9)?
   b) How were the Christians in the first century experiencing this war on a more personal level?

6. Explain Satan's title "accuser of our brothers" (12:10). (See Job 1:10.)

Day 3

7. a) How do Christians defeat Satan (12:11)? (See 1:9; Mark 16:17-18; Heb 12:2-4.)
   b) Give an example of some victory over evil you have seen in your own life.

8. How are the eagle's wings and the desert signs of God's providence for the Church (12:14)? (See Exod 19:4; Deut 32:11; Jer 2:2; Hos 2:16-17.)

9. What does the beast from the sea represent (13:1-7)? (See 17:3-10.)

Day 4

10. What is the connection between Nero and the head that is wounded and healed (13:3)?

11. a) What would "fascinate" the whole world to follow the beast (13:3)? (See Col 2:8; 2 Pet 2:1-3.)
    b) How does one combat this kind of fascination?

12. What practice is represented by the beast from the earth (13:11-14)? (See 19:20; Matt 24:24.)

Day 5

13. a) What is the interpretation of 666 (13:18)?
    b) Why would Christians have spoken in such a secretive manner?
    c) How has this symbolic number been misused or misinterpreted in more recent times?

14. Why does the author emphasize a "new hymn" (14:3)? (See 5:9; 13:12.)

15. What do adultery and virginity mean in biblical symbolism (14:3-4)? (See Isa 1:21; Jer 2:2; 3:3; Ezek 16:23; Hos 1:2.)

Day 6

16. Why is Babylon used to speak of God's judgment (14:8)? (See 18:1-24; Isa 21:9; Jer 51:1-59; Dan 4:27-28.)

17. a) What is the underlying message about punishment in 14:10-11? (See 20:10; Isa 34:9-10.)
    b) How can knowledge of hell be both a help and a hindrance in serving God (14:11-12)?

18. What does wielding the sickle represent (14:14-19)? (See Isa 63:1-6; Joel 4:13; Amos 8:2; Matt 13:36-43.)

LESSON 7   Rev 15–17
CBC-NT volume 11, pages 63–69

Day 1

1. What was particularly challenging to you in last week's lecture?

2. How does the "song of Moses" apply to the vision found in 15:1-4? (See Exod 15:1-18.)

3. What images in 15:5-8 are particularly impressive to introduce the vision of God's wrath?

Day 2

4. Which Egyptian plagues are reflected in the first three bowls of wrath (16:1-4)? (See Exod 7:17-18; 9:8-11.)

5. Why is water turning to blood viewed as a suitable punishment (16:6)? (See Ezek 35:6.)

6. Why do some continue to rebel against God against all odds (16:9-11)? (See Amos 4:6.)

Day 3

7. What does the image of the thief (16:15) tell us about calculating the date of the end of the world? (See 3:3; Matt 24:42-44; 1 Thess 5:1-4; 2 Pet 3:10.)

8. In what ways can you live in readiness (16:15)?

9. What is meant by Armageddon (16:16)? (See 2 Kgs 23:29-30; Zech 12:11.)

Day 4

10. Point out the standard apocalyptic symbols in the destruction described in 16:18-21.

11. Who is the great harlot (17:5, 18)?

12. How have the kings of the earth committed fornication with the harlot (17:2)? (See 14:4.)

Day 5

13. What is meant by the statement that the beast "existed once but exists no longer, and yet it will come again" (17:8)? (See 13:3.)

14. How does 17:9 make clear that the vision is indeed about Rome?

15. Why are there several groups of kings mentioned in the vision (17:9-12)?

Day 6

16. When is the harlot defeated by the Lamb (17:14)?

17. How do the wicked kings help promote God's plan (17:16-17)?

18. In many ways, the power of evil has come to a climax in the description of Babylon in these chapters. In what ways could the label "Babylon" be applied to our own civilization today?

LESSON 8   Rev 18–20
CBC-NT volume 11, pages 69–79

Day 1

1. What images from the previous lesson evoked fear? What evoked hope?

2. What did ancient Babylon symbolize for the Jews (18:2)? (See Ps 137:8; Isa 39:6; Jer 20:6; 50:18; 51:35-37.)

3. a) Identify the characteristics of "Babylon" found in 18:1-3.
   b) How does the modern Christian "depart from Babylon" (18:4)? (See Gen 19:12-13; Num 16:26; Rom 12:2; Eph 5:1-5.)

Day 2

4. How can you reconcile the vengeful tone of 18:6-7 with Jesus' advice in Matt 5:38-48?

5. What are the reactions of the kings, merchants, and sailors to the fall of Babylon (18:9-19)?

6. a) How much do economic interests influence your lifestyle and decisions? Your religious observance?
   b) Comment on the saying "The love of money is the root of all evils" (1 Tim 6:10). (See Matt 6:24.)

Day 3

7. Sailors and others were said to mourn the loss of the "great city" (18:18). Over what dreams and plans have you mourned?

8. The words of the angel express utter desolation (18:21-24). What words or images would you choose to speak of such desolation?

9. a) What is the literal meaning of "alleluia," the song of the heavenly assembly (19:1-4)? (See Ps 150.)
   b) Do you think it significant that "Alleluia" is only found here in the New Testament? Why?

Day 4

10. When is the wedding day of the Lamb (19:7-9)? (See 21:2; Matt 22:1-14; Mark 2:19.)

11. Contrast the dress of the bride, the Church (19:8) with that of the harlot of 17:4.

12. How does the rider of 19:11-16 differ from the riders in 6:1-8?

Day 5

13. What are the titles of the rider in 19:11-16?

14. Trace the biblical pictures of birds as instruments of divine punishment or as agents of profanation in Gen 40:19; 1 Sam 17:43-44; 1 Kgs 14:11; Isa 18:6; Bar 6:21; 2 Macc 9:15; 15:33.)

15. What period of time is meant by the "thousand years" (20:2-6)?

Day 6

16. a) What is the first resurrection (20:5-6)?
    b) What would be the "second resurrection"?

17. What is meant by Gog and Magog (20:8)? (See Ezek 38–39.)

18. "All the dead were judged according to their deeds" (20:13). What motivates the deeds of your life?

LESSON 9 Rev 21–22
CBC-NT volume 11, pages 79–85

Day 1

1. What do you want to remember from last week's discussion or lecture?

2. a) How is 21:1-4 a proclamation of the fulfillment of Jewish hopes? (See Ezek 40:1-2; 43:1-9; Zech 2:5-17.)
   b) What is the meaning of "a new Jerusalem" for Christians?

3. Meditate on the truth, "God's dwelling is with the human race" (21:3). How does this make you feel? (See Matt 1:23; John 1:14.)

Day 2

4. How does the author attempt to convey heaven's loveliness (21:9-21)? (See Exod 35:4-9; Tob 13:16-17.)

5. What symbolic functions do the patriarchs and apostles serve in the heavenly city (21:12-14)? (See Isa 28:16; Matt 21:42; Acts 4:11; Eph 2:20; 1 Pet 2:4-7.)

6. a) What is the temple in this city (21:22)?
   b) What other meanings of "temple of God" are found in the New Testament? (See 3:12; Mark 12:35; John 2:19-21; 1 Cor 6:19; 2 Cor 6:16; Eph 2:21.)

Day 3

7. In what ways has the Church served as a light to the nations (21:24)? (See Isa 42:6; Matt 5:14-16; Luke 2:31-32.)

8. How do we drink at the river of life-giving water now (22:1-2)? (See Ps 1:3; Isa 55:1; Ezek 47:1; John 4:14.)

9. What, in simple terms, is the "prophetic message" of this book (22:7)? (See 1:3.)

Day 4

10. What does it mean to say "the appointed time is near" (22:10)? (See Mark 1:15; John 12:31; Acts 17:31.)

11. When is it most difficult for you to persevere in holiness (22:11)? (See Col 2:6-7; James 1:2-4.)

12. How is Jesus both "the Root and the Offspring of David" (22:16)? (See Isa 11:1; Matt 22:41-46; Rom 15:12.)

Day 5

13. Which season of the Church year is especially appropriate for the prayer "Come, Lord Jesus" (Maranatha) (22:20)?

14. From chapter 22, list the titles of
    a) God the Father
    b) Jesus
    c) the Holy Spirit
    d) the Church.

Day 6

15. What is the most striking difference between the vision of the "new Jerusalem" (21:9–22:5) and that of "Babylon" (17:1–18:24)?

16. What is the most significant understanding you have gained from the Book of Revelation?

17. How can the Book of Revelation be a source of hope for Christians today?

NOTES